Benjamin Hooks

African-American Leaders

Carol Moseley-Braun

Henry Louis Gates, Jr.

Benjamin Hooks

Eleanor Holmes Norton

Condoleezza Rice

Cornel West

AFRICAN-AMERICAN LEADERS

Benjamin Hooks

Heather Lehr Wagner

CHELSEA HOUSE
PUBLISHERS
A Haights Cross Communications Company
Philadelphia

CHELSEA HOUSE PUBLISHERS
VP, New Product Development Sally Cheney
Director of Production Kim Shinners
Creative Manager Takeshi Takahashi
Manufacturing Manager Diann Grasse

Staff for BENJAMIN HOOKS
Editor Sally Cheney
Editorial Assistant Josh Spiegel
Production Editor Megan Emery
Photo Editor Sarah Bloom
Series & Cover Designer Terry Mallon
Layout Jennifer Krassy Peiler

A Haights Cross Communications ⭐ Company

www.chelseahouse.com

First Printing

1 3 5 7 9 8 6 4 2

Library of Congress Cataloging-in-Publication Data

Wagner, Heather Lehr.
  Benjamin Hooks / by Heather Lehr Wagner.
    p. cm. — (African American leaders)
Includes index.
Summary: A biography of African American lawyer Benjamin Hooks, who continues to
speak and teach about racial justice and equality since his 1992 retirement from the
position of executive director of the NAACP.
  ISBN 0-7910-7685-7
  1. Hooks, Benjamin L. (Benjamin Lawson), 1925—-Juvenile literature. 2. African
American civil rights workers—Biography—Juvenile literature. 3. Civil rights work-
ers—United States—Biography—Juvenile literature. 4. National Association for the
Advancement of Colored People—Biography—Juvenile literature. 5. African American
lawyers—Tennessee—Memphis—Biography—Juvenile literature. 6. African American
clergy—Tennessee—Memphis—Biography—Juvenile literature. 7. African Americans—
Civil rights—History—20th century—Juvenile literature. 8. United States—Race rela-
tions—Juvenile literature. 9. Memphis (Tenn.)—Race relations—Juvenile literature. [1.
Hooks, Benjamin L. (Benjamin Lawson), 1925- 2. Civil rights workers. 3. Lawyers. 4.
Clergy. 5. African Americans—Biography. 6. African Americans—Civil rights—
History—20th century. 7. National Association for the Advancement of Colored
People.] I. Title. II. Series.
  E185.97.H774W34 2003
  323'.092—dc22

                                                                    2003016553

Table of Contents

Introduction

Beginning with the publication of the series *Black Americans of Achievement* nearly twenty years ago, Chelsea House Publishers made a commitment to publishing biographies for young adults that celebrated the lives of many of the country's most outstanding African Americans. The mix of individuals whose lives we covered was eclectic, to say the least. Some were well known—Dr. Martin Luther King, Jr., for example—although others we covered might be lesser known—Madam C.J. Walker, for example. Some—like the actor Danny Glover—were celebrities with legions of adoring fans. It mattered not what an individual's "star" quality might be, or how well known they were to the general public. What mattered was the life of the individual— their actions, their deeds, and, ultimately, their influence on the lives of others and our nation, as a whole. By telling the life stories of these unique Americans, we hoped to tell the story of how ordinary individuals are transformed by extraordinary circumstances to people of greatness. We hoped that the special lives we covered would inspire and encourage our young-adult readers to go out in the world and make a positive difference; and judging from the many wonderful letters that we have received over the years from students, librarians, and teachers about our *Black Americans of Achievement* biographies, we are certain that many of our readers did just that!

Now, some twenty years later, we are proud to release this new series of biographies, *African-American Leaders,* which we hope will make a similar mark on the lives of our young-adult readers. The individuals whose lives we cover in this first set of six books are all contemporary

African-American leaders. As these individuals are all living, the biographers made every attempt to interview their subjects so they could provide first-hand accounts and interesting anecdotes about each subject's life.

After reading about the likes of Henry Louis Gates, Jr., Cornel West, Condoleezza Rice, Carol Moseley-Braun, Eleanor Holmes Norton, and Benjamin Hooks, we think you will agree that the lives of these African-American leaders are remarkable. By overcoming the barriers that racism placed in their paths, they are an example of the power and resiliency of the human spirit and an inspiration to us all.

The Editor
Chelsea House Publishers

1

Power and Passion

> "I want you [NAACP members] to know that the struggle that we will face... through the twenty-first century will not be an easy one. It is fraught with pitfalls and plagued with setbacks, but we as people have developed a resiliency which has made it possible for us to survive slavery and various discrimination. We must never tire nor become frustrated.... We must transform stumbling blocks into stepping stones and march on with the determination that we will make America a better nation for all...."
>
> —Benjamin Hooks, *Let Freedom Ring*

On the evening of April 3, 1968, Martin Luther King, Jr., arrived at the Masonic Temple in Memphis, Tennessee. He was speaking before a smaller crowd than some of the large gatherings he had addressed in recent months, and the audience was eagerly anticipating an inspiring speech in preparation for the large march that King and others were organizing for April 5.

King had come to Memphis to demonstrate that civil disobedience—a nonviolent response to injustice—could work. The organization with which King was associated—the Southern Christian Leadership Conference (SCLC)—had rapidly seized the nation's attention for its civil rights protests in the 1960s. There were other organizations that were working to right the historical discrimination against African Americans—groups like the National Association for the Advancement of Colored People (NAACP) and the Congress of Racial Equality (CORE)—but the SCLC was notable for its role as the center of the nonviolent protest movement.

The SCLC was made up principally of African-American ministers, many of whom were affiliated with the Baptist church. Their view of nonviolent protest as the best way to spark change was unpopular, even among many leading African-American activists of the 1960s, but King argued at every opportunity that civil disobedience—things like protest marches, sit-ins, and other peaceful demonstrations—would be more effective to spark change within a city and a society than more violent demonstrations or riots.

But King's goal of nonviolent protest was not always effective. On a trip to Memphis a few weeks earlier, he had seen how difficult it was to keep pent up the strong passions built on generations of oppression.

A STRIKE IN MEMPHIS

In February 1968, more than a thousand sanitation workers in Memphis had called for a strike to protest dangerous working conditions—two workers had been fatally crushed in a garbage-packing machine—and their lack of workers' compensation benefits. Most of the sanitation workers were African Americans. The mayor of Memphis, a segregationist (someone who believes in separating racial groups from each other) named Henry Loeb, labeled the strike illegal and warned the workers that they would be replaced if they did not immediately return to work. Many of the strikers and their supporters (including several well-known African-American clergymen) were attacked with clubs and mace during a march. Some leading members of the Memphis African-American community asked Dr. King for his assistance.

When King arrived in Memphis, he agreed to participate in a protest march on the City Hall. The protest, taking place on March 28, 1968, attracted some 5,000 participants. But the march quickly spun out of control, and many protestors stopped marching and began to break windows and loot shops in the center of town. It was a major embarrassment to King and the SCLC, and the FBI soon launched an investigation to see precisely why the violence had occurred and whether or not the SCLC was responsible.

King made it clear that the SCLC had not organized the march, but that he remained committed to supporting the striking sanitation workers. He promised to return to Memphis to lead another nonviolent demonstration, this time one the SCLC would itself organize.

The second march was scheduled for April 5, and it was this that had brought King to Memphis when he spoke to the Masonic Temple audience. He spent a good part of that April 3 meeting with the groups that had organized the march of a few weeks earlier—the one that had culminated in violence—stressing that they must commit themselves to a nonviolent approach to the civil rights movement. He argued that all groups must commit to ensuring that violence did not break out again and was rewarded with their eventual agreement. Then, King proceeded to the Masonic Temple for his speech.

He had received several threats prior to his arrival—in fact, his flight to Memphis had been delayed by a bomb threat—and King dwelled on these during his speech. Many who were in the audience believe that this speech, delivered on April 3, 1968, in Memphis, was his finest, most passionate talk ever. King noted that he had survived an attempt on his life when a racist had tried to stab him some ten years earlier. He rarely discussed this assassination attempt and yet, on this night, he spoke of it at some length and then noted that now, he no longer cared what happened to him:

> "We've got some difficult days ahead. But it really doesn't matter with me now, because I've been to the mountaintop.... And I've seen the Promised Land. I may not get there with you. But I want you to know tonight that we as a people will get to the Promised Land. And I'm happy tonight. I'm not worried about anything. I'm not fearing any man. Mine eyes have seen the glory of the coming of the Lord."

The audience immediately jumped to its feet. They were clapping and cheering. Many were weeping.

PROTEST AND POLITICS

In the audience on that electrifying night was a member of the SCLC who was involved in Memphis politics, both as a protestor and as a political figure. Benjamin Lawson Hooks had been gaining attention since 1949 as one of the few African-American lawyers in Memphis. He was also an ordained Baptist minister who preached at Memphis' Middle Baptist Church. In 1965, he had become

11

the first African-American criminal court judge in Tennessee history.

But Hooks was also an active participator in protests in the Memphis area, and it was his involvement with the SCLC that had drawn him to the Masonic Temple that April evening.

In later years, Hooks would remember King's speech vividly.

> "As I sat there that night, I thought never had I heard him speak with such pathos, power, and passion," Hooks recalled several decades later. "This was 1968, and we thought we had come a long way.... Yet on that night, Dr. King talked about dark and difficult days ahead.... But he did not leave us in despair or hope-lessness."

For Hooks, King's words would prove both prophetic and inspiring. King left that speech that April evening happy and relaxed. He spent the night with his brother and friends, and slept in until noon the following day. One of his advisers, Andrew Young, arrived in the afternoon to deliver the welcome news that the city's attempt to stop the march had been denied.

Around 6:00 P.M., King dressed for dinner—he had been invited to the home of Reverend Billy Kyles. King stepped out on the balcony of his motel. A shot rang out. James Earl Ray, waiting at the rear bathroom window of a rooming house opposite King's motel, had fired at the civil rights leader. Within minutes, King was dead. But the movement he had founded, the dream he had shared with a nation, would continue.

Many would carry on the crusade for civil rights that King helped launch. Some would choose violence; others

This 1968 photograph of civil rights leader Martin Luther King, Jr. was taken just one day before his assassination. King's message of change through nonviolent civil disobedience was an inspiration for so many Americans, including Hooks. From left to right are Hosea Williams, Jesse Jackson, King, and Ralph Abernathy.

political activism; still others would use moral arguments to appeal to the conscience of Americans.

They would all find the truth in King's speech in Memphis: There is much to be done, much that will be difficult, but there have been successes and more will come.

13

Like many of his fellow civil rights activists in 1960's America, Benjamin Hooks was inspired by the powerful words of Dr. Martin Luther King, Jr. Hooks's dedication to the cause of racial equality began much earlier, however, growing up in segregated Memphis, Tennessee and serving in a segregated U.S. military during World War II.

Benjamin Hooks was one of those, inspired by the examples of King and others, to continue to work for change. "The civil rights movement is not dead," Hooks stated in 1977. "If anyone thinks that we are going to stop agitating, they had better think again. If anyone thinks that we are going to stop litigating, they had better close the courts. If anyone thinks that we are not going to demonstrate and protest... they had better roll up the sidewalks."

But for Benjamin Hooks, the fight for equality and civil rights began long before Martin Luther King, Jr.'s speech in Memphis, or his assassination the following day. It had its roots in a Memphis family committed to pursuing excellence, no matter what the cost. It had its roots in a childhood spent coping with segregated bathrooms, water fountains, and restaurants, and military service in World War II where the prisoners Hooks was guarding were frequently able to eat in restaurants where he was not allowed.

The life of Benjamin Hooks shows how one man, determined to change injustice, can transform the society around him. It is an inspiring story of how hard work, persistence, personal sacrifice, and a willingness to fight wrongs helped to bring about a new era in civil rights.

2

The Struggle in Tennessee

"Thank God for Julia Ann Amanda Moorhead Britton Werles Hooks, and for the man who founded this school, his legacy, and for his belief in the fact that we are all children of one God. And so to you, young people of Berea College, a great heritage has been passed, a great legacy is yours ... and I hope that we all will leave here today, determined to do our best to uphold the best standards of living."

—Benjamin Hooks,
2002 Berea College Founders Day speech

On January 31, 1925, a son was born to Robert and Bessie Hooks. He was the fifth child in a family that would eventually grow to seven children. Benjamin Lawson Hooks may not have been Robert and Bessie Hooks's first child, but he would spend much of life achieving many "firsts"— including becoming the first African American elected to a criminal court judgeship in Tennessee and the first African American appointed to the Federal Communications Commission in Washington, D.C.—while fiercely and tirelessly fighting to ensure greater equality for others.

But these accomplishments would take many years and much hard work to achieve. The revolution in which Hooks would participate—a revolution that would dramatically change the opportunities available to African Americans—was a distant dream in segregated Memphis, Tennessee, when Hooks was born.

Tennessee had long wrestled with its legacy as a state that had a history of containing—and condoning—a separate society for African Americans. Tennessee had entered the Union in 1796 at a time in United States' history when slavery was expanding. Tennessee soon became a state that relied on slave labor, particularly in the western part of the territory. By 1860, slaves made up approximately one-fourth of Tennessee's total population.

Laws were soon passed to protect what had become an economically important institution. There was some opposition to slavery within Tennessee, especially in the early part of the nineteenth century, and there were attempts to abolish slavery in the state. But these were voted down, in large part because of an inability of those opposed to slavery to offer a clear-cut plan to ensure that the state's economic prosperity would continue if such a large percentage of its slave labor was freed.

There were a small number of free blacks living in Tennessee, but as concerns about the success of abolitionists (those attempting to bring an end to slavery) in other states began to affect policymakers, laws were passed to ensure that their numbers remained small. In 1831, free blacks were barred from immigrating to Tennessee, and slave owners were barred from setting their own slaves free unless they had made arrangements to remove them from the state. Free blacks had initially held the right to vote in Tennessee, but this right was taken away from them by a constitutional convention held in 1834. In 1854, yet another law was passed that required that freed slaves be quickly transported out of the state and, in fact, out of the country—to West Africa.

The first half of the nineteenth century clearly brought about great changes in the rights given to African Americans in Tennessee. The Civil War brought even greater changes. Following the war, Tennessee was presented with a preliminary proclamation from President Lincoln, in which he outlined his intention to free all slaves in 100 days. The actual Emancipation Proclamation was issued by Lincoln on January 1, 1863 and said, in part:

> ... on the 1st day of January, A.D. 1863, all persons held as slaves within any State or designated part of a State the people whereof shall then be in rebellion against the United States shall be then, thenceforward, and forever free: and the executive government of the United States, including the military and naval authority thereof, will recognize and maintain the freedom of such persons and will do no act or acts to repress such persons, or any of them, in any efforts they may make for their actual freedom.

Andrew Johnson, a Union loyalist and supporter of Lincoln's policies, was named the military governor of Tennessee in 1862. Jonhson would find himself faced with the difficult task of enforcing the Emancipation Proclamation. There was strong opposition to the policy, as well as President Lincoln's mandate that Tennessee would only be readmitted to the Union once slavery had been abolished. It was only in 1865, following Lincoln's reelection (with Johnson as his running mate) that a more cohesive post-war policy toward the issue of slavery began to be formed.

THIRTEENTH AMENDMENT

In April 1865, the General Assembly of Tennessee met and ratified the Thirteenth Amendment to the Constitution. The amendment stated, in part:

Neither slavery nor involuntary servitude, except as a punishment for crime whereof the party shall have been duly convicted, shall exist within the United States, or any place subject to their jurisdiction.

The assembly also examined and adjusted some of the legal codes that had governed the rights of African Americans in Tennessee; however, most of the men creating these laws were former slave owners. The new laws were still quite restrictive: contracts between African Americans and whites had to be witnessed by whites, and African Americans could testify only in court cases involving other African Americans. Later legal actions repealed the policy restricting the ability of African Americans to testify in court against whites, but this action was passed only when accompanied by an addendum that noted that African Americans could not attend all-white schools or serve on juries. By 1866, as part of an effort to ensure Tennessee's readmission into the Union, additional rights had been granted, guaranteeing African Americans the right to sue (or be sued) and to inherit property.

Voting rights were the next focus. African Americans in Tennessee had been petitioning for the right to vote as soon as the Civil War had ended, and when Tennessee was readmitted into the Union in 1866, leaders of the state's African-American community organized the State Equal Rights League as part of their campaign to obtain the right to vote. On February 5, 1867, their efforts were successful, as Tennessee became the second state outside New England to give African Americans the right to vote.

These policies had been passed while the Unionist-supported Radical Party was in power, but when that party lost political power to the Democrats, the rights of African Americans began to slip as well. The Radical Party had passed laws challenging segregation; these were repealed under the Democrats. The Tennessee Constitution of 1870 mandated segregation in the state's public school system, and outlawed interracial marriage. Racially motivated attacks by the Ku Klux Klan (a terrorist organization founded in the South following the Reconstruction period) soon began to threaten African Americans. Appeals by the African-American leadership to the national authorities in Washington to come to their aid went largely unanswered.

The Fourteenth Amendment to the Constitution states, in part:

> All persons born or naturalized in the United States, and subject to the jurisdiction thereof, are citizens of the United States and of the state wherein they reside. No state shall make or enforce any law which shall abridge the privileges or immunities of citizens of the United States; nor shall any state deprive any person of life, liberty, or property, without due process of law; nor deny to any person within its jurisdiction the equal protection of the laws.

The Fifteenth Amendment offers its own clear mandate to address voting rights:

The right of citizens of the United States to vote shall not be denied or abridged by the United States or by any state on account of race, color, or previous condition of servitude.

Despite these clear mandates, the 1870s were marked by numerous complaints by African Americans that Tennessee was failing to enforce these two amendments to the Constitution. Approximately one-quarter of the population of the state of Tennessee (the African-American citizens) were practically unable to effect any change in their political status.

CHANGE IN MEMPHIS

By the 1880s, African Americans in West Tennessee, particularly in the Tenth Congressional District (the district containing the city of Memphis), began to grow tired of being ignored, discriminated against, and denied equal opportunities. In certain portions of the southwestern section of Tennessee, African-American votes made up fifty percent or higher of the eligible voters, and they were determined to become better organize, at the grass-roots level, to ensure that their voices were heard. A key focus was the public school system, to ensure that African Americans were given access to the appropriate state educational facilities and that their schools were staffed with competent teachers and scheduled for full terms.

Ultimately, in the 1880s, 12 African Americans were elected to serve in the Tennessee legislature—they were lawyers, businessmen, schoolteachers, and a minister. Most had previous public service experience. They focused on challenging racial segregation in public transportation, on the unequal distribution of funds used for public education, and spoke out against the violent, racially motivated attacks occurring in the state.

These twelve legislators motivated other African Americans to work toward using the political channels available to them. Although little change occurred on the state level, other African Americans continued to organize political action on the local level. In Memphis, this created a backlash, when white groups began to counter-organize, creating political movements based on opposition to African-American political power.

In 1880, African Americans made up approximately 45 percent of the population of the city of Memphis. Political parties either wooed African-American voters or, failing to receive their support, quickly reverted to crude attempts at invoking racial fears. It is important to understand how intensely race began to play an issue in the political process in Memphis. Consider this comment from the Memphis newspaper, the *Avalanche*, published on December 2, 1889: "In the South the Democratic party stands for pure government and for white government; the Republican party represents corruption and ignorance.... [the Democratic candidates] do not ask nor expect the votes of the negroes. They ask for white votes and they expect to get them and plenty of them."

With this clear attempt to draw racism into the political process, it is not surprising to note that segregation gradually became more prevalent in Memphis as the nineteenth century drew to a close. Increasingly, African Americans were not welcome at certain hotels, at certain theaters or in certain sections of theaters, or in certain public parks. One woman refused to accept this policy—that, having bought a ticket to the theater, she could not sit where she chose. That young woman was Benjamin Hooks's grandmother, Julia Britton Hooks.

EDUCATIONAL OPPORTUNITIES

Julia Amanda Britton was born in Frankfort, Kentucky, in 1852. It quickly became clear that she was a musical prodigy, and she began performing in public, playing the piano, at the age of five. At the age of eighteen, she became one of the first African-American women in Kentucky to attend college when she enrolled at Berea College.

Berea College was founded in 1855 by an abolitionist, Reverend John G. Fee, who was supported in his efforts by grants from the American Missionary Association and a wealthy antislavery politician who lived in Kentucky's Madison County, Cassius M. Clay. Clay provided Fee with ten acres in southern Madison County to set up an anti-slavery church, the Glades Church. Two years later, the church added a school. The school was designed to, in the words of its constitution, "furnish the facilities for a thorough education to all persons of good moral character, and at the least possible expense, and all the inducements and facilities for manual labor which can reasonably be supplied.... This College shall be under an influence strictly Christian, and as such, opposed to Sectarianism, Slaveholding, Caste, and every other wrong institution or practice." While other colleges admitted African-American students in the 1800s—including Cheyney State College and Lincoln University in Pennsylvania and Wilberforce University in Ohio—Berea was noteworthy for its stated purpose of bringing African-American and white students together, both to learn and to work side by side. It is even more noteworthy when we consider that Kentucky, in which the college was founded, was a state that allowed slavery.

Reverend Fee had chosen the name "Berea" for his college after a biblical town whose residents were open-mind-ed and tolerant. He wrote a pamphlet, the "Antislavery Manual," and soon he and his colleagues were preaching their abolitionist message to the people of western Kentucky. By the winter of 1859, local slave owners had organized and, in December, 65 armed men rode into Berea and ordered Fee to leave the state within ten days. Fee and his colleagues took their case to the governor of Kentucky, but he refused to provide them with protection. The members of the Berea community were forced to flee out of the state.

When the Civil War began, many members of the Berea community were able to slip back into Kentucky, and among them was John Fee. He began preaching to and teaching slaves who were volunteering to serve in the Union Army at Camp Nelson. Camp Nelson was an immense site, stretching across some 4,000 acres and containing more than 300 buildings and fortifications. More than 10,000 African-American soldiers were recruited and trained there, making it the third largest recruiting and training depot for African Americans in the nation. Thousands of African Americans gained their freedom at Camp Nelson, and many of them also brought their families with them.

Gradually, Camp Nelson established a refugee camp at the base for these families, and the American Missionary Society, an abolitionist group founded just before the war broke out, soon sent missionaries to administer to the families at the camp. Among these was Reverend John Fee, who arrived at the camp in 1864. Fee's philosophy of racial equality, and his desire to educate the freed slaves to become independent, self-reliant members of an integrated American society, found fertile soil in the atmosphere at Camp Nelson. Near the camp, Fee eventually formed the settlement of Hall and Ariel College, both of which were based on the ideals Fee had first detailed at Berea.

When the war ended, Fee returned to Berea and began reestablishing an interracial college and a new church that would focus on combating prejudice. Fee invited some of the soldiers he had taught—and their families—to join him at Berea and continue their education, and by 1870, just at the time that Julia Britton had arrived, Berea had become an interracial town, with churches and Berea College at its center.

Some 200 African-American families settled in the area around Berea. The majority of the students at the college were either from the area or boarded with families living there. Fee further emphasized his policy of encouraging an interracial community by buying up large tracts of land in the area and then reselling them as housing lots along racially integrated patterns, so that African Americans and whites would live together as neighbors. This was all to reenforce the school's motto: "God has made of one blood all peoples of the earth."

The students and faculty were encouraged to improve not only themselves, but the community in which they lived. Campaigns were organized to build better housing for the community, to improve school buildings, to increase the books available for home and school libraries, to increase public school funding, and to build better roads. The Southern Appalachians became a focus for much of the efforts of Berea College students. Work programs were organized in the most economically depressed parts of this region for students to continue their service.

The education—both within and outside the classroom—had a ripple effect on the community and the state of Kentucky. In 1878, the college's president cited a figure of at least 100 schools at which African-American teachers who had been educated at Berea taught.

The faculty of Berea College was also interracial. In fact, Julia Britton was the first African-American faculty member of the college, combining study with serving as a teacher of instrumental music. From 1870 to 1872, she taught at the school. She was joined there by her sister, Mary E. Britton, who was three years younger. Mary studied at Berea from 1871 to 1874, two years longer than Julia, who graduated from Berea in 1872. By doing so, she became the second African-American woman in the United States to graduate from college.

Julia eventually moved to Memphis, marrying Charles Hooks. Charles Hooks worked as a truant officer. His wife continued her passionate interest in music, becoming active in such musical groups as the Liszt Mullard Club, which performed classical music concerts in Memphis during the 1880s. Her musical skills also led her to involvement with various churches in the city, where she played the organ and directed choirs and choral groups. She also taught music, and her students gave recitals each year at Memphis' Zion Hall and the Beale Street Baptist Church.

By 1881, Julia Hooks was also working as a teacher in the Memphis public schools. She had earned a reputation as a tireless worker, a dedicated teacher, and a skilled pianist, all of which placed her at the forefront of Memphis' African-American society. She soon added one more facet to her reputation: civil rights activist.

In March 1881, Julia Hooks attended a performance in a Memphis theater. Memphis had been struggling under increasing pressure to segregate public facilities, and this particular theater had recently buckled under the pressure. In years past, Julia Hooks and other African Americans had been able to sit in the main section of the theater for any performance. But on this occasion, Mrs. Hooks was directed to a so-called "colored balcony," instead of the main section where she normally sat. Mrs. Hooks ignored the request and instead went and sat in the section of the theater that was now reserved for white patrons.

Mrs. Hooks refused to move, even when the police were called. She was ultimately carried from the theater by two policemen and then arrested for disorderly conduct. A trial before a local magistrate followed, where it was revealed that the policy of segregation was only recently installed in the theater. In the past, Julia Hooks and other African Americans testified, they had been able to sit in the main section of the theater, and in fact even during the 1881 season they were allowed to sit in the main section when the theater was not crowded.

But the theater manager testified that it was his belief that anyone was guilty of disorderly conduct if they sat in a section where they were not supposed to sit and refused to move. Apparently, the magistrate agreed, for at the trial's end Mrs. Hooks was fined five dollars.

THE ANGEL OF BEALE STREET

Julia Hooks would gradually combat the problem of segregation in Memphis's public schools—and the resulting inequality of facilities, skilled teachers, and resources offered to African-American children—within the system (as a teacher and principal), and still later by opening her own private kindergarten and elementary school. These were operated in her home on Memphis' South Lauderdale Street. Her sons, Henry and Robert, were among her earliest students.

She was an inspiring teacher who inherently understood

27

Julia Britton Hooks, Benjamin's grandmother, was an extraordinary woman—musical prodigy, the first African-American faculty member of her alma mater, Berea College, and civil rights activist—Julia Britton Hooks did it all. Out of her concern for the needy in Memphis, she founded an Orphans and Old Folks Home and became known as "The Angel of Beale Street."

children and how best to motivate and inspire them. In addition to her classes and music lessons, she organized plays, musical programs, and even picnics. Musical recitals would often be a cause for celebration when Mrs. Hooks arrived with an ice cream cone for every student.

Gradually, Mrs. Hooks turned her attention to children at risk. She became an officer of the Juvenile Court, offering counseling and advice to children in trouble, as well as providing spiritual counseling to adult prisoners she encountered.

In 1907, Memphis opened a small juvenile detention facility next to the Hooks' home, which Julia and her husband supervised. Tragically, Julia's husband was killed by one of the young men they were attempting to help, but Julia continued her work. She became so admired for her dedication and the success of her work that a Memphis judge in the juvenile court system, Camille Kelly, often asked Mrs. Hooks to sit in on court cases involving young African Americans.

In 1909, Mrs. Hooks became a charter member of the National Association for the Advancement of Colored People (NAACP). Her grandson, Benjamin Hooks, would later describe her as "born to rebel."

Julia Hooks founded the Old Folks and Orphans Home, raising money for its operation from concerts in which she herself performed. She also founded the Hooks School of Music in Memphis. She eventually became known as "The Angel of Beale Street" for her work with underprivileged members of Memphis' society.

Julia Hooks lived her beliefs, and her family and descendants shared her sense of duty and passion for equal rights. Her sister, Mary Britton, after graduation from Berea College, taught at several schools from 1876 to 1897. She too became active in civil organizations in Kentucky, serving as a secretary to the board for the Colored Orphans Home and becoming the founding director of the Colored Orphans Industrial Home. Mary Britton was involved in the suffrage (votes for women) movement, and served as the president of the Lexington women's improvement club. She also wrote hundreds of newspaper articles protesting racial segregation, which were published in such newspapers as the *American Citizen*, the *Lexington Leader*, and the *Daily Transcript*. Mary Britton eventually decided to go back to school, ultimately graduating from the American Missionary College. She then returned to Lexington, Kentucky, where she became the first African-American woman to practice medicine in that city. For nearly 20 years she worked as a physician while also remaining active in social causes.

A NEW GENERATION

This passion for justice and achievement was passed on to the next generation. Julia's two sons, Henry and Robert, both became talented photographers, establishing their own photography studio known as Hooks Brothers Photographers. They became active in Memphis politics and society, and their children would hold jobs as civil servants, educators, and politicians.

Julia Hooks lived to be ninety years old, playing the piano until only a few weeks before her death. She died in 1942, but her life continued to inspire her grandson, Benjamin Hooks.

"What trials, what travails, what tribulations we have seen," he said. "Yet my grandmother had this great sense of duty, and of education."

The importance of duty, and of education, that was ingrained in Berea College students created a sense of responsibility. The challenges that faced African-American students in Julia Hooks's day were clear. In 1890, less than 20 percent of male or female African Americans aged 15 to

20 attended school of any kind—high school or college. Perhaps more disturbing is the fact that nearly half of all African-American men and women in that same age group were illiterate.

Benjamin Hooks learned, from the example of his grandmother, that equal opportunity did not come easily. Her alma mater, Berea College, founded to provide a place where people of all races could learn and work together, was forced to buckle to the new segregationist legislation passed in the early 1900s. Following a bitter, four-year struggle, the Supreme Court, in *Berea College* v. *Commonwealth of Kentucky*, ruled in 1908 that the state could require a private institution to segregate students of different races. African-American students were forced to leave the campus, and the college whose motto was "God has made of one blood all peoples of the earth" would be segregated until 1940.

3

Childhood
in Memphis

"The magnificent manner in which our service
personnel comported themselves in early 1991, displaying discipline, initiative, intelligence, and techno-
logical competence, is truly commendable. Black
servicemen and women, like all of their colleagues,
share in the glory and the nation's pride. The real test,
however, is how we treat them when they return. They
have every right to expect of their Commander-in-
Chief [President George H.W. Bush] the kind of
courageous leadership in civilian life he gave them
during war time. They have every right to expect his
full support of a Civil Rights Act in 1991 that reme-
dies the retrogressive decisions of the Supreme Court.
They have every right to expect his Administration to
lead an all-out assault on our domestic ills with the
same energy and commitment which was expended to

greet the people of Kuwait and defeat Iraq's cruel dic-
tator. In 1991, the NAACP will make certain the
nation does not forget these essential truths."
—Benjamin Hooks,
A compendium of thoughts and excerpts
from the Executive Director of the NAACP
on the significant issues of our time

When Benjamin Hooks was born in 1925, his parents
were considered fairly well off by their Memphis
neighbors. Robert Hooks's photography studio was successful, and it generated enough income to provide the
family with a fairly comfortable life. But only a few years
after Benjamin's birth, the Depression struck, and economic change quickly came to Memphis and to the Hooks family.

Hooks's earliest childhood memories are of this difficult period for the family. He wore the hand-me-down
clothes from his three older brothers, and his mother,
Bessie Hooks, was forced to plan and prepare meals that
would stretch the groceries enough to feed a family of nine.
"We were better off than many," Hooks said. "We always
had something to eat."

As Hooks's memory notes, the Depression crippled
many families in Memphis. The city had undergone some
dramatic changes since the nineteenth century. The city
had grown larger in population and more modern in
appearance. As increasing industrial and commercial business began to influence the city's development, new buildings replaced the old. By 1914, many of these businesses
were housed in skyscrapers; a new city hall and police station had been built. Class divisions, as well as racial divi-

Benjamin's parents, Robert and Bessie Hooks (pictured here), provided a stable and nurturing home in Memphis for their children. Robert Hooks owned a photography studio that sustained his large family, even during the difficult economic times of the Depression.

sions, were clear—the wealthy industrialists and business-men lived in grand homes, and conspicuous consumption marked the years before the Great Depression struck.

But increasing urbanization, and increasing wealth, also brought increasing resentment, and this frequently erupted in violence. African Americans were often the target of attacks, most often by poorer whites. In 1900, "Wild Bill" Latura, a poor owner of a shabby bar in Memphis, walked into an African-American saloon one day and killed six of the customers there. It was a sign of the general attitude in the city that few people in Memphis wanted to see Latura charged with any crime. In fact, shortly after being arrested, he was set free.

The newspapers in Memphis published outrageous

criticisms of President Teddy Roosevelt in 1901, when he invited Booker T. Washington to lunch at the White House. While some white citizens, frequently members of the clergy, spoke out in condemnation of lynching (hanging or otherwise killing without any legal authority, often by a mob targeting an African American), the general attitude among the white community in Memphis toward African Americans was, at best, that they were somehow inferior.

Much of Memphis's development in the early part of the 20th century was shaped by its mayor, Edward H. Crump. Elected in 1910, he immediately began a series of civic improvements that included persuading railway officials to construct street underpasses. He ensured that railroads and utilities, which previously had benefited from general deals by political allies, paid their fair share of taxes.

✐ Crump also focused on law and order issues. He had promised voters that he would rid the city of much of the crime that had made it a violent place to be, and nearly twice as many arrests were made in 1910 as had been made in 1909. But African Americans soon became the target of what, today, we would describe as racial profiling. Every African American found on the streets of Memphis after midnight was arrested. African Americans were routinely seized if they unfortunately happened to be in the vicinity of where a crime had been committed. One of the most horrific examples of this occurred in May 1917, when a sixteen-year-old white girl was assaulted and murdered just outside the city limits. A mentally handicapped African American was quickly arrested. He was removed from the city to await trial, but a mob, carrying guns, quickly tracked him down and demanded that the policeman guarding him hand him over, which they did. A mob of some 500, in cars and on foot, assembled at the place where the girl had been murdered, and the suspect was quickly brought to the spot and burned before being dismembered.

There was little public protest against this display of mob violence, of a violation of the civil liberties that a country on the brink of World War I claimed to value so highly. The Memphis of the early part of the 20th century, despite displaying so many signs of progress, was still crippled by prejudice.

MEMPHIS IN THE 1930s

Memphis in the 1930s was still a city in transition. Race relations continued to be difficult. Many, like Julia Hooks, had determined to devote their lives to fighting for greater opportunities for people of color and to helping those less fortunate. Others chose to speak out, using political and other public forums to protest the indignities African Americans were suffering.

But while many chose to protest, others chose to simply accept the injustice with which they were confronted on a daily basis. This decision—to temporarily accommodate the policies in place—meant that segregation quickly became the rule—in schools, in parks, in restaurants, and hotels.

The Hooks family was not willing to suffer in silence. Robert Hooks was stern and strict, and both Robert and Bessie worked hard to ensure that their children set high goals and then achieved them.

"So many today have a harum-scarum life," Hooks recalled in a 1976 interview in the *Washington Post*. "But because of that training I have a fairly disciplined life. That's why I get a lot done."

A sense of service was demonstrated by all older members of the Hooks family. Julia Hooks was a clear example to all of her grandchildren, but young Benjamin also saw from the examples of family members and family friends

This photo taken in 1927 shows young Benjamin, his mother Bessie, and his five brothers and sisters. Although Hooks recalls his childhood years as being difficult for his family economically, he admits that they were better off than most families in Memphis. Here we see Bessie Hooks (seated) holding Benjamin's sister, Mildred. Standing left to right are young Benjamin, brother Raymond, sister Julia, cousin Ethel, brother Charlie, and brother Robert.

that being relatively well-off meant that they had a responsibility to help out those less fortunate. He also gained from their example an understanding that there was also a duty to fight for greater rights for African Americans. Hooks felt that he belonged to "sort of a militant family"—his older sister worked as a secretary in the Memphis branch of the NAACP during a period of time when simply joining that organization was viewed as risky.

In addition to a responsibility to serve their community, the Hooks children were also expected to earn good grades and to attend college. Robert and Bessie Hooks made it clear that segregation would not be an excuse to prevent their children from great accomplishments.

Segregation was a fact of life in the Memphis of Hooks's childhood. The schools that Hooks attended were segregated—Porter Elementary School and Booker T. Washington High School. He was limited to facilities labeled "colored only"—water fountains, bathrooms, and restaurants.

Despite Robert Hooks's distaste for organized religion, Benjamin Hooks was drawn to religion. One of his earliest mentors was the Reverend G.A. Long, who invited activist A. Phillip Randolph to speak at his church.

Asa Philip Randolph was one of the most visible spokespersons for African-American rights from the 1930s to the 1950s. He helped to launch the Brotherhood of Sleeping Car Porters, and the union soon won the support of the NAACP, the American Federation of Labor, and the National Urban League for its efforts to provide African Americans with respect and a livable wage.

Randolph was born in Crescent City, Florida, in 1889. His parents were both descendants of slaves. He graduated from Cookman Institute, the first high school for African Americans in Florida; then in 1911 he traveled to Harlem, secretly hoping to become an actor. Instead, he took classes at City College and then joined the Socialist party and became involved in politics. In 1917, Randolph helped to establish a radical African-American magazine called *The Messenger.*

Randolph was brought in to head The Brotherhood of Sleeping Car Porters in 1925 by members of the union who feared that their employer, the powerful Pullman Company, might retaliate against them for union activities. Randolph was chosen because he was not a porter, but also because of his speaking skills and his reputation for fighting for the rights of African Americans. For 12 years, Randolph struggled with Pullman before finally winning their agreement to negotiate with the union; in 1937 his efforts were finally rewarded when the Pullman Company signed a contract with the Brotherhood—the first contract ever between a company and an African-American union.

In the 1940s and 1950s, Randolph continued to speak out for African-American rights, this time focusing on such national issues as the number of African Americans needing public assistance and discrimination in defense industry hiring. Randolph organized a March on Washington to demand that African Americans be given access to defense industry jobs, winning a concession from President Roosevelt that banned discrimination within the government and among defense industries receiving government contracts.

Later, Randolph clashed with President Truman, demanding that segregation be eliminated from the military. He organized a protest, calling for African Americans to refuse to register for the draft or serve if called. On July 26, 1948, President Truman issued an executive order barring discrimination in the military.

Randolph remained a leading figure in the civil rights

movement. When he died in 1979, his funeral was attended by many leading political figures, including then-president Jimmy Carter.

But in segregated Memphis, before Randolph had won many of the rights listed above, then-mayor Ed Crump had prohibited Randolph from speaking at the church Hooks attended. But Reverend Long was determined to allow Randolph to speak. Hooks was a member of the audience during that speech as Memphis fire marshals arrived on the mayor's orders to try and close the church to prevent Randolph from speaking.

Reverend Long refused to back down, outlasting his opponents in Memphis, who eventually labeled him as "crazy" and decided to leave him alone. The experience taught Hooks that, by refusing to be dominated, a determined activist might outlast the segregationists—although at the risk of being called names. "That's what they did with people they couldn't handle," Hooks said. "... dismissed you as crazy, to restore their manhood."

Benjamin Hooks was a shy young man, but he was deeply impressed by the example of the charismatic Reverend Long and decided that he might want to pursue a career in the ministry. Robert Hooks quickly convinced him that this was not a wise choice. Instead, he took his son with him to the office space he shared with other African-American professionals. Benjamin Hooks listened to these lawyers and doctors speak, and eventually decided that a career in the law might be a good fit for him.

In 1941, Hooks graduated from Booker T. Washington High School and enrolled in Memphis's LeMoyne College. For two years, he studiously worked through the pre-law program, occasionally worrying that his shyness would

Growing up in Memphis, Hooks (seen here in his high school graduation portrait) attended segregated public schools. After graduating from Booker T. Washington High School in 1941, Hooks enrolled in Memphis's LeMoyne College, where he studied pre-law.

prove too great an obstacle in his chosen career; at other times worrying about the expense to his parents of his attending law school after college.

These worries were soon unexpectedly put to rest. World War II had broken out, and Benjamin Hooks was drafted into the U.S. Army.

SERVING HIS COUNTRY

Many scholars feel that World War II was one of the most decisive events in the campaign for civil rights. At the time that the war broke out, African Americans comprised approximately 10 percent of the U.S. population. By drafting Hooks and other African Americans, the U.S. government made it clear that they had a responsibility to serve their country. It is not surprising, then, that after the war these veterans would note that if they were required to serve their country as equals, then they expected that country to *treat* them as equals.

To better understand the military climate in which Hooks found himself, it is important to understand that African-American participation in the military just before America entered World War II was quite small. In 1939, there were only 3,640 African-American soldiers in the U.S. Army, and only five African-American officers, three of whom served as chaplains. In the Navy, African Americans were only allowed to serve in the galleys. African Americans served only in very small numbers in the Coast Guard and were not allowed to serve at all in the Marines or Army Air Corps (the predecessor to the Air Force).

It was African Americans who lobbied to change this, arguing that there should not be any form of discrimination in either the way military personnel were selected or in the way they were trained. Segregation had been rampant within the military, even to the point of requiring separate on-base facilities such as post offices, canteens, and theaters. Civilians at southern bases frequently insulted African-American soldiers as they trained to serve their country.

In December 1941, the executive secretary of the NAACP, Walter White, wrote to General George C. Marshall, the U.S. Army's Chief of Staff. White urged Marshall to consider the idea of a volunteer Army division that would be "open to all Americans irrespective of race, creed, color, or national origin." White believed that this type of military unit would clearly illustrate the ideals of American democracy. But the military was not interested in White's proposal.

First Lady Eleanor Roosevelt also chose to speak out on the unfair treatment of African Americans by the military. "The nation cannot expect the colored people to feel that the U.S. is worth defending if they continue to be treated as they are treated now," Mrs. Roosevelt said only a few days after the attack on Pearl Harbor. "I am not agitating the race question," she explained. "The race question is agitated because people will not act justly and fairly toward each other as human beings."

The war forced many to take a harsh look at what place segregation could have in a country that claimed to believe that "all men are created equal." Stories of Nazi segregation of Germany's Jewish population carried disturbing echoes of the segregation of African Americans in the South. Roy Wilkins, former head of the NAACP, noted the irony in his autobiography *Standing Fast*:

> America was so accustomed to setting the Negro outside any moral and ethical consideration that the country had been going about its business as if no conflict existed between its high pronouncements and its practices.... Black people wanted nothing new or startling. They were asking nothing they had not asked for before Hitler came to power, nothing inconsistent with the declared war aims of the United States, nothing inconsistent with the Constitution and the Bill or Rights. They were asking simply for complete equality: equality before the law, equality in security of person, equality in human dignity. Negroes did not need us at the NAACP to tell them that it sounded pretty foolish to be against park

benches marked JUDE in Berlin, but to be for park benches marked COLORED in Tallahassee, Florida. It was grim, not foolish, to have a young black man in uniform get an orientation in the morning on wiping out Nazi bigotry and that same evening be told he could buy a soft drink only in the 'colored' post exchange.

Wilkins pointed out that segregation, rather than the Axis powers, might be the greatest obstacle the American military would face in World War II. African-American soldiers who had agreed to serve their country in fighting against a system practicing racial genocide were forced to wait several months to be inducted, simply to allow the military time to build separate facilities for them. At training camps they were required to live separately, ride separate buses, buy their candy and cigarettes at separate counters, and attend movies in separate theaters.

The Selective Service Act, signed by President Franklin D. Roosevelt on September 14, 1940, had served to reinforce this policy. A. Philip Randolph, whom Hooks had heard speak in Memphis, had attempted to meet with President Roosevelt prior to his signing of the act to request that he change some of the Act's language, but Randolph's request was refused. The act stated that no man would be inducted "until adequate provision shall be made for shelter, sanitary facilities, medical care and hospital accommodations." This language was largely interpreted to mean that the military would be segregated by race, and indeed, as Wilkins had noted, many African Americans who attempted to enlist were turned away due to a lack of adequate segregated facilities.

But the First Lady chose to speak out against the policy, attending (in the same month that her husband signed the act) the convention of Randolph's Brotherhood of Sleeping Car Porters. Following the meeting, Eleanor Roosevelt urged her husband to reconsider the issue of segregation in the military. Eventually, he relented, and Randolph and others were invited to meet with the president and his assistant secretary of war.

On October 9, 1940, the White House announced a new policy, with mixed results for African Americans. The new policy promised that the number of African Americans in the Army would be increased to better reflect their percentage of the population, that African-American combat and noncombat units would be organized in all branches of the military, including the Air Corps and Marines, and that African Americans would be given the opportunity to attend officer training schools. But the policy also stated that all officers in all African-American units—with the exception of the three African-American regiments already in place—would be white. And while both African Americans and whites would be given the same opportunity to serve their country, they would still be segregated into separate regiments.

THE "DOUBLE V"

Segregation was also being practiced by defense contractors, and as those industries geared up to fulfill wartime contracts, the promise of jobs in those industries was frequently denied to African Americans. This was the next target for A. Philip Randolph. In 1941, Randolph determined to organize a march on Washington for July 1, to protest discrimination in hiring policies by any defense contractors being used by the U.S. government. Nearly 100,000 marchers were mobilizing when, less than a week before the march, President Roosevelt signed Executive Order 8802,

forbidding discrimination in industries holding government contracts for war production and establishing the
Fair Employment Practices Commission, which gave the
government the power to take action against discrimination.

Despite these actions, discrimination still became a factor that affected African-American perceptions of the war
effort. When the Red Cross launched a blood drive, African
Americans frequently found themselves turned away from
contributing. As Washington, D.C., geared up for home-
front defense by preparing air-raid shelters, many were dis-
turbed to learn that it was deemed necessary to build separate shelters for African Americans and whites. Race riots
frequently broke out during the war, particularly when
African-American soldiers attempted to use the same facilities as their fellow GIs who happened to be white.

The idea of a "Double V" campaign began to spread
throughout the African-American community. The idea
was that a war was being fought on two fronts—one against
the Axis powers, and the other against racism in the U.S.
Two victories were hoped for (the "double V")—one resulting in the defeat of Hitler, the other in the defeat of discrimination.

Benjamin Hooks's wartime service clearly illustrated
the irony of a war fought against religious intolerance by a
country practicing racial intolerance. At a U.S. Army base
in Georgia, Hooks was assigned the task of guarding Italian
prisoners of war. But these prisoners of war were allowed to
eat in restaurants in Georgia that were off limits to
Hooks—because of the "for whites only" signs in the window.

When the war ended, Hooks was discharged from the
army. He had earned the rank of staff sergeant. He, like

Hooks's law school aspirations were put on hold when he was drafted into the Army during World War II. Seeing the racial inequalities between whites and African Americans in the service, Hooks became even more committed to pursuing a career in law. Sadly, after the war, Hooks would be denied admittance to law school in Tennessee and would have to travel north to DePaul University in Chicago to pursue his dream of attending law school.

many other African Americans, had been willing to serve his country. But that country now refused to give him the same rights as other white Americans were receiving.

Hooks was determined to pursue his dream of becoming a lawyer. But Staff Sergeant Hooks immediately encountered an obstacle. No law school in his home state of Tennessee

4

The Law and Communication

"Any political profit from playing the race card is hardly worth the exacerbation of racial tension. What is troubling about the rise of black conservatives is their seeming obliviousness to the long history and the contemporary prevalence and pervasiveness of racism. We have seen before that conservative black spokespersons are used to validate white notions of appropriate race relations. Remember, in 1895 Booker T. Washington solemnly pledged that blacks and whites could be "separate as the fingers" in the sphere of social interaction. A year later, the Supreme Court issued the "separate-but-equal" ruling in *Plessy* v. *Ferguson*."

—Benjamin Hooks,
A compendium of thoughts and excerpts
from the Executive Director of the NAACP
on the significant issues of our time

Benjamin Hooks, having been denied the opportunity to study law in his native Tennessee, decided to head north. The G.I. Bill, designed to help military veterans, helped cover some of the cost of his law school tuition. In 1946, he enrolled at DePaul University in Chicago, where he earned his J.D. degree in 1948. Trips back and forth between home and law school provided vivid reminders of how crippling segregation could be. "I wish I could tell you every time I was on the highway and couldn't use a restroom," Hooks said in *U.S. News and World Report.* "My bladder is messed up because of that. Stomach is messed up from eating cold sandwiches."

When Hooks graduated from DePaul in 1948, he considered several lucrative job offers in Chicago. But he decided to return instead to Memphis, determined to help bring an end to the policy of segregation.

He passed the Tennessee bar examination, but found few doors open to him. "I could not get a job as an assistant public defender, assistant county attorney or an assistant prosecutor—the kinds of things that many lawyers do to make a living while they are getting their practices established," Hooks said.

Instead, Hooks decided to open up his own legal practice. Quickly, he found himself confronted with prejudice and bigotry. "At that time you were insulted by law clerks, excluded from white bar associations and when I was in court I was lucky to be called 'Ben.'" Hooks later recalled in an interview with *Jet* magazine. "Usually it was just 'boy.' [But] the judges were always fair."

The courts of Memphis were segregated in 1949, when Hooks began his law practice. The few African-American lawyers in the city were not allowed to join the white bar associations or use the law library. They even had to use separate bathrooms in the courthouse.

Memphis was not alone in presenting an inhospitable climate for African-American lawyers. In 1940, there were only 1,925 African-American lawyers in the entire United States—in essence one African-American lawyer for every 13,000 African Americans. Before 1949, there were no African-American judges on the United States Circuit Court. Before 1936, African Americans could not be admitted to "white" law schools, and these same law schools did not have African-American faculty members before 1946. Up until 1943, applicants to the American Bar Association were required to state their color on their application.

Many African-American attorneys, like Hooks, found themselves isolated professionally. There were few opportunities to work with white lawyers, and fewer still to represent white clients. The idea of bias against African-American lawyers pleading a case before a white judge or arguing a case against a white lawyer led many African-American clients who needed legal representation to choose a white lawyer. Even in 1963, U.S. Secretary of Labor Willard Wirtz still saw a problem, describing the legal profession as the worst segregated group in the whole economy.

A NEW CALLING

In 1949, as one of the few African-American lawyers in Memphis, Benjamin Hooks had begun to make a name for himself. Attending the Shelby County Fair that summer, he met a pretty 24-year-old teacher named Frances Dancy. They began to date, and Frances was impressed by the "good looking, very quiet, very intelligent" young lawyer. "He loved to go around to churches and that type of thing," she said, "so I started going with him. He was really a good catch."

After a few months of dating, the couple decided to become engaged. They were married on March 21, 1951. They later adopted a daughter, Patricia.

Hooks remained committed to opposing and ending segregation. When the NAACP organized boycotts of businesses and restaurant sit-ins in Memphis in the late 1950s and early 1960s to protest discriminatory policies, Hooks frequently participated. Remembering the restaurant sit-ins, Hooks recalled, "I was always served—sometimes sullenly, but I was served."

Hooks also served on the board of the Southern Christian Leadership Conference (SCLC), an organization founded by Dr. Martin Luther King, Jr. The organization united people from different political, social, religious, and ideological backgrounds with one goal—to support nonviolent activities that challenged racism.

While the SCLC was founded on principles of love and understanding, it frequently encountered neither during its attempt to spark change. Its campaign of nonviolent direct action often was met with violent response on the part of those opposed to changing the policies of segregation that dominated daily life, particularly in the South. The SCLC organized demonstrations, marches, boycotts, and sit-ins as a response to discrimination.

The SCLC contained many African-American ministers, since they had often been at the forefront of addressing the needs of their community. Clergymen frequently played a role in establishing churches and outreach services to the community, and they saw the potential offered by the SCLC and supported King's philosophy of social advancement and justice through nonviolent direct action.

It is not surprising to learn that Hooks began to reconsider the calling he had once felt to the ministry once he became a member of the SCLC. He decided to pursue the calling, and was ordained as a Baptist minister, all the while continuing his legal practice. He became the pastor of the Middle Baptist Church in Memphis in 1956. In 1964, he also became the pastor of the Greater New Mount Moriah Baptist Church in Detroit. He flew to Detroit twice a month to conduct services.

Hooks also attempted to effect change from within the system, launching unsuccessful campaigns for the state legislature in 1954, and for juvenile court judge in 1959 and 1963. But the shy young man had become an outgoing presence in the Memphis legal community, and in his campaigns Hooks attracted not only African-American supporters, but some liberal white supporters as well. He was even endorsed, in the 1963 campaign, by the Memphis daily newspaper the *Commercial Appeal.*

In 1961, he was appointed assistant public defender of Shelby County (the county in which Memphis is located). In 1965, the governor of Tennessee, Frank G. Clement, appointed Hooks to fill a vacancy in the Shelby County criminal court—thereby making Hooks the first African-American criminal court judge in Tennessee history.

JUDGING HISTORY

In 1966, Benjamin Hooks ran for election to a full term as Shelby County criminal court judge; the one-year vacancy he was filling was set to expire. This time, he was elected.

Hooks found that the experience of preaching in the pulpit helped him overcome his inherent shyness. Although he is frequently described as soft-spoken in one-on-one conversations, from the pulpit his speeches were often passionate, delivered in ringing tones. Hooks borrowed from the speaking styles of King and other Baptist preachers he admired.

"Some intellectuals feel ashamed of the Southern Baptist tradition," Hooks said in 1977. "To me that is insincere. Blacks have a rich tradition in speaking and singing."

For several years, Hooks combined his responsibilities as a judge, a lawyer, and a minister. He also continued to participate in civil rights protests and marches organized by the NAACP and the SCLC. But by 1968 he was exhausted from juggling so many different tasks. On December 31, 1968, Hooks resigned his seat on the criminal court bench. He wanted to devote his time and energy to his ministries—and to a new task. He had been asked to assume the presidency of Mahalia Jackson Chicken Systems, Inc., a fast-food chain.

Unfortunately, Mahalia Jackson Chicken Systems went out of business after two years. But Hooks had also become involved in the media, working on three Memphis television series. He produced and hosted the program *Conversations in Black and White*, co-produced the program *The 40 Percent Speak* (the title came from the fact that 40 percent of Memphis's population was African American), and served as a panelist on the program *What is Your Faith?*. It was this media role that would lead him to a much bigger position on the national stage.

THE FCC

In 1968, Republican Richard Nixon was a candidate for the presidency. One of his campaign promises in that election year was to appoint the first African American to the Federal Communications Commission, the office of the government that licenses and regulates radio and television stations, as well as telephone, telegraph, and satellite communications.

When Nixon was elected, he was not allowed to forget this particular campaign promise. African-American media coalitions and the Congressional Black Caucus had filed complaints, charging that African Americans were being unfairly portrayed by the media and being discriminated against in matters of license granting and renewals.

Hooks had supported the Republican ticket during the 1968 campaign and this, combined with his legal background and experience in Memphis television, brought him to the attention of President Nixon. On April 12, 1972, Richard Nixon announced that Benjamin Lawson Hooks was his nominee to succeed FCC Commissioner Robert T. Bartley, who was retiring from the seven-member commission. The Senate confirmed the nomination, and on July 6, 1972, Benjamin Hooks was sworn in as the first African-American appointee to the FCC.

Benjamin and Frances Hooks moved to Washington, D.C. Frances had earlier recognized that her husband's activism would require sacrifice on her part. She had given up her career as a teacher and guidance counselor to serve as her husband's assistant, adviser, and secretary. As she later explained in an interview in *Ebony*, "He said he needed me to help him. Few husbands tell their wives that they need them after 30 years of marriage so I gave it up and here I am. Right by his side."

Hooks's successful nomination to the FCC was a result of extensive lobbying by such African-American organizations as the Black Efforts for Soul on Television (BEST). Before his nomination, there had been no minority representation on the FCC, and only two women—Frieda

Henncock and Charlotte Reid—had held seats on the seven-member commission. Also responsible for his nomination was the Kerner Commission's "Report of the National Advisory Commission on Civil Disorders," which had been published in 1968 following research into ways to address the civil unrest that had marked much of the 1960s. The Kerner Commission's report had included a section labeled "The Negro in the Media," which had recommended that African Americans be integrated "into all aspects of televised presentations."

Most African-American organizations working with the media believed that the best way to ensure that African Americans were accurately and positively depicted by the media was to ensure that they were represented on the commission that governed broadcasting—the FCC. For this reason, Hooks's appointment carried with it heavy baggage—intense expectations on the part of certain groups that his appointment would quickly lead to greater opportunities for African Americans in the media.

The FCC was created by an act of Congress on June 19, 1934, to merge the administrative responsibilities for regulating broadcasting and wired communications under a single agency. The FCC has the power to license operators of the various services it regulates, to assign station frequencies and power, to classify stations and prescribe their services, to approve equipment and mandate standards for acceptable levels of interferences, to make regulations for stations with network affiliations, to prescribe qualifications for station owners and operators, and to levy fines and order stations to cease operation if they are in violation of FCC regulations.

During Hooks's tenure, the FCC viewed as part of its

mandate the responsibility to provide radio and television station licensees with clear guidance as to what constituted adequate public service. This was a markedly different philosophy from the "marketplace" rationale that later governed FCC policies—the idea of licensing many different stations in a given area to provide consumers with a choice, based on the idea that competition would better ensure that stations provided adequate public service.

COMMISSIONER HOOKS

While Hooks's appointment was, in part, Nixon's response to demands by BEST and other African-American organizations that he honor his campaign promise, Hooks was in many cases not their first choice as candidate for the position. Hooks was one of three African Americans who had been considered for the appointment; leaders of BEST did not think that Hooks was as qualified as one of the other candidates—Ted Ledbetter, a communications consultant based in Washington, D.C. The third candidate for the position was an attorney from New Orleans named Revius Ortique.

BEST initially objected to Hooks on the grounds that he did not have enough broadcasting experience. But the fact that Hooks was not an industry insider made him more attractive to those groups that were also outside the communications industry. Such groups as The National Media Coalition, Citizens Communications Center, and the United Church of Christ all believed that their cases would receive a fair hearing because of Hooks's presence on the commission, believing that a commissioner from outside the broadcasting industry would ensure that organizations previously removed from broadcasting policymaking would at last get access.

Hooks was widely viewed as someone who would serve as a representative for the interests of minorities in broadcasting policies. At times, these expectations were justified, but Hooks was determined to judge cases on their merits. In several instances, he was forced to take a stand that was unpopular with the very groups he was expected to represent. One of the most difficult involved a case in which a political candidate for the U.S. Senate from Georgia, J.B. Stoner, had produced and aired a series of radio and television ads as part of his primary campaign that referred to African Americans as "niggers." Protests were quickly filed with the FCC, requesting that they ban the offensive commercials. Hooks, however, believed that the First Amendment guarantee of free speech protected Stoner, and he refused to vote for a ban, arguing that it would ultimately prove more harmful to African Americans and other groups if the commercials were pulled, rather than allowing them to air and give a clear expression of the candidate's views. "Even if it hurts sometimes, I'm a great believer in free speech and would never do anything to tamper with it," Hooks said in the *New York Times.*

Yet another challenging decision came when Hooks and the other FCC commissioners heard a case involving Equal Employment Opportunities (EEO) and the broadcasting industry. Before 1976, stations that had more than four employees were required to file a report that categorized the number of employees by race and gender. But in 1976 the FCC proposed to change this policy, suggesting instead that only certain larger stations would be required to file this type of statistical report. However, the FCC's policy specified that an EEO program would outline ways to increase minority representation at these stations.

The decision sparked protest by groups that felt that this FCC proposal would mean decreased pressure on smaller stations to hire minorities. Hooks was petitioned by the protestors to declare his opposition to the policy but he refused, stating his belief that the new regulations would, in fact, prompt the hiring of more women and minorities by larger stations. However, Hooks did oppose the portion of the policy that removed the requirement for stations with fewer than 50 employees to file EEO reports.

Hooks did believe that minorities needed to become more actively involved in radio and television. He said, "Until we become part of the image-making process we are foredoomed to failure."

During his tenure as a member of the FCC, he focused on ensuring that the cause of minority ownership of radio and television stations was supported. His legacy included the establishment of an office of Equal Employment Opportunity at the FCC, an increase in the number of African Americans employed at FCC offices, and an increase in the number of minorities employed in broad-casting.

Benjamin Hooks served five years of his seven-year term at the FCC before a new opportunity led him in a new direction. Roy Wilkins was stepping down as president of the NAACP. The organization wanted Benjamin Hooks to become its new president. Hooks left the FCC, noting that he planned to continue his commitment to advancing the cause of minorities in broadcasting by establishing a com-munications department in the NAACP "to see how we can make television more responsive to the people, black and white."

But other, more pressing issues needed to be addressed first. The NAACP was an organization in crisis. And

Benjamin Hooks needed to ensure that it still had a place in the civil rights movement.

5

The NAACP

"Americans are far more willing to acknowledge and respect talent on the football field, the basketball court, and the baseball diamond than in the class-room, the laboratory, the halls of government, and the financial centers of the nation. Sports are important in the life of America. Sports provide entertainment and relaxation to millions. Millions live vicariously through the success of teams and stars. Yet, racism still pervades much of professional sports. Many believe that blacks are under-represent-ed in the so-called "thinking positions" of the sports. It is time for a rededication of effort to the principle that sports, a great equalizing force in our society, will, more and more, represent our best ideals of unity and fair competition."

—Benjamin Hooks,
A compendium of thoughts and excerpts
from the Executive Director of the NAACP
on the significant issues of our time

On November 6, 1976, Benjamin Hooks was elected executive director of the National Association for the Advancement of Colored People (NAACP) by the 64 members of the NAACP's board of directors. The election was effective on the date of the retirement of then-director Roy Wilkins some nine months later.

Between the time of his election and his actual induction into office, Hooks issued several public statements to clarify his positions on the areas that he felt should become the focus of NAACP action. He made it clear that the NAACP was not, in his opinion, an outdated organization (as some had charged). He tackled affirmative action—a policy in which employers and schools, among others, consider race and gender in potential candidates to improve hiring and educational opportunities for women and minorities.

Hooks promised to tackle what he perceived as inequitable hiring policies in government offices, in the print media, and noted that affirmative action was the "only workable, humane means" to deal with "handicaps growing out of centuries of black exclusion." Hooks also warned that "white folks had better understand that we're going to enjoy it [the American dream] too, or, like the flies, we're going to make sure nobody enjoys it."

As Hooks prepared to assume leadership of the NAACP, the renowned civil rights organization was in trouble. Younger African Americans were charging that the NAACP was no longer in step with the times, and that more militant groups like the Black Panthers were better able to respond to the needs of the African-American community. Hooks's challenge was to make sure that the historic organization continued its mission while remaining responsive to a changing climate.

Benjamin Hooks was elected executive director of the National Association for the Advancement of Colored People (NAACP) in 1976. Intent on keeping the NAACP as a viable organization, Hooks became committed to fighting for affirmative action. Here we see Hooks with Coretta Scott King (center) and Doris Edwards at an NAACP convention in 1980.

A HISTORICAL PERSPECTIVE

The NAACP was founded in 1909 in response to violence—a race riot in Springfield, Illinois, the hometown of Abraham Lincoln. The riot had injured 80, and in its violent outburst two African Americans had been lynched and six had been fatally shot. A white reporter for the *New York Evening Post*, Mary White Ovington, read an account of the events by a wealthy socialist reporter from Kentucky, William English Walling. She became determined to take action.

Ovington invited Walling to a meeting at her New York apartment where, joined by liberal social worker Dr. Henry Mosciwitz, they determined to fight for the rights of African Americans. They invited influential African-American activist W.E.B. Du Bois to join their movement. On May 31, 1909, nearly 300 prominent educators, economists, anthropologists, and philosophers gathered to form what was initially called the National Negro Committee, promising to work to improve the lives of African Americans.

Nearly a year later, on May 5, 1910, the committee voted to change the name of their organization to the National Association for the Advancement of Colored People. The organization, to be based in New York City (later it would be moved to Baltimore), would focus on providing legal aid, organizing meetings, and investigating injustices. Initially, the NAACP's officers were all white, with Moorfield Story, a white Boston lawyer, serving as its first president. Soon, W.E.B. Du Bois was brought on board to serve as chairman of the executive committee, focusing his efforts on research and publicity.

Eventually, the NAACP began to publish its own magazine, called *The Crisis*. Editor W.E.B. Du Bois intended *The Crisis* to serve as a vehicle for recording events that affected the lives of African Americans; he wanted it to provide a review of racial issues; he also used it as a forum for his own editorials on issues pertinent to African Americans. The magazine quickly sparked a crisis of its own between white and African-American members of the NAACP, who viewed the magazine's content and editorial style quite differently. Many white members believed that *The Crisis* veered too close to propaganda with its inflammatory prose; African Americans loyally supported it and the major African-American universities soon began to advertise in its pages.

W.E.B. Du Bois did not focus exclusively on white targets. His editorials criticized the education provided by Wilberforce University, an African-American school; he targeted the African-American press and the African-American church. It soon became clear that the NAACP's expectation that *The Crisis* would serve as a publicity vehicle for the organization was at odds with the more militant goals of its editor. White members of the NAACP were concerned by Du Bois's refusal to publish reports of crimes committed by African Americans and by his labeling of any criticism as racially biased.

A split began to develop between white and African-American members of the NAACP. Many, including Mary White Ovington, began to wonder whether whites had a role to play in the struggle for racial equality, or whether African Americans should fight this battle on their own.

As membership in the NAACP continued to grow, it began to focus increasingly on combating the violence against African Americans being committed by the Ku Klux Klan (KKK), by lynchings, and by race riots. As much of the lynching was taking place in the South in the years following World War I, an effort was made by NAACP field secretary James W. Johnson to increase NAACP presence in the southern United States. African Americans also began to assume key leadership positions in the NAACP. James Weldon Johns was the first African American to be named an NAACP secretary, in 1921.

NAACP efforts to build a campaign of public awareness about the horrors of lynching and other racially based violence were largely responsible for prompting

Congress to take action. In 1919, the NAACP published a report that documented the violence, titled *Thirty Years of Lynching in the United States, 1889–1918.* A year later, the U.S. House of Representatives attempted to pass an anti-lynching bill, but Southern Democrats were able to prevent its passage. Nonetheless, the NAACP viewed the attempt as evidence that its activities were beginning to effect change.

BROWN V. BOARD OF EDUCATION OF TOPEKA

One of the NAACP's greatest political actions came in the 1950s, when the Reverend Oliver Brown challenged the Topeka, Kansas, board of education and its claim that it was providing "separate but equal" schools for both white and African-American students. The Brown family lived only seven blocks from an elementary school, but that school was for whites only. Reverend Brown's young daughter, Linda, was forced to walk six blocks (taking her across a dangerous railroad yard) to a bus stop, then ride that bus for one hour and 20 minutes, and then wait a half-hour before the elementary school that was for African-American children opened.

The NAACP helped to ensure that this challenge to segregation traveled through the court system, eventually supporting it all the way to the U.S. Supreme Court in 1954. The NAACP established a Legal Defense and Education Fund, designed to challenge "separate but equal" laws and instances of educational discrimination. School systems in Kansas, South Carolina, Virginia, Delaware, and Washington, D.C., were all challenged by the Legal Defense and Education Fund.

By the time *Brown v. Board of Education of Topeka* reached the Supreme Court, it actually represented the consolidation of five separate cases challenging the "separate but equal" ruling, including the initial case brought by Reverend Brown. The Supreme Court ultimately found that "separate but equal" did not provide minority children with equal educational opportunities. The case was viewed as a triumph for the civil rights movement, and for the NAACP, even thought it did not immediately end segregation in school.

In 1955, Roy Wilkins—an African-American activist who had replaced W.E.B. Du Bois as editor of *The Crisis* and then served in various leadership roles—became the executive director of the NAACP. He ensured that the NAACP worked hard to guarantee that states complied with the *Brown* decision. The actions resulted in frequent threats against NAACP members.

Roy Wilkins was born in St. Louis, Missouri, in 1901. He grew up in a low-income, integrated community in St. Paul, Minnesota, living with his aunt and uncle. Wilkins worked his way through the University of Minnesota, holding a number of jobs, including stockyard worker and editor. He graduated in 1923 and then joined the staff of the *Kansas City Call*, a weekly newspaper for African Americans. He joined the local chapter of the NAACP, soon serving as the chapter's secretary.

His leadership skills brought him to the attention of the national organization, and he became the assistant executive secretary of NAACP leader Walter White. When W.E.B. Du Bois stepped down as editor of *The Crisis*, Roy Wilkins became its editor. He was one of a group of leading African Americans chosen to serve as advisers at the 1945 conference in San Francisco that led to the founding of the United Nations. Upon White's death in 1955, Wilkins became the executive secretary of the NAACP.

Wilkins believed strongly in legislative reform as a tool to achieve civil rights, feeling that violence and separatism (popular among many younger African Americans) were not the right approach to achieving equality. Wilkins served in the administration of President Lyndon Johnson as an adviser and later was a consultant to Presidents Nixon, Ford, and Carter.

Wilkins's moderate approach made him the target of criticism by more militant groups, underscoring their argument that the NAACP was outdated. His achievements, including overseeing the NAACP's efforts to provide legal and financial support to "ghettoized" urban areas, were frequently overshadowed by criticism of his support for using more democratic processes to achieve change. He stepped down in 1977 and died in 1981.

While Wilkins was its leader in the 1960s, the NAACP became involved in sit-ins and protests against restaurants and businesses in the South that segregated customers or placed "whites only" signs in their establishments. But the NAACP focused more on sparking change through legal action and legislation. This was in contrast to the campaigns of such groups as Martin Luther King, Jr.'s SCLC, which attempted to effect change through grass-roots movements and nonviolent direct action. Some younger members believed that the NAACP's methods were outdated, and Wilkins was even forced to suspend the president of the NAACP's Monroe, North Carolina, office, Robert Williams, when he called for the NAACP to meet "violence with violence."

A NEW CRISIS

In the years just before Benjamin Hooks was named its director, the NAACP faced new challenges. The types of discrimination it now needed to combat were less overt, and the NAACP needed new strategies to fight them. The NAACP shifted its focus to promoting affirmative action, to challenging unequal use of the death penalty (in which African Americans convicted of crimes were more often sentenced to death than whites), and to ensure that the civil rights records of judges (particularly Supreme Court nominees) were considered during the confirmation process. The NAACP also focused on challenging media bias—in movies, radio, and television.

But the organization faced a critical challenge just before Hooks assumed office. The controversy surrounded a 1976 Mississippi court case in which Robert Moody, a state highway patrolman, had been awarded $250,000 in a lawsuit against the NAACP. Moody claimed that local and state NAACP officials had slandered and libeled him when they charged him with police brutality, claiming that he had beaten an African American during an arrest for drunk driving. The NAACP was forced to borrow money to post the bond, although the judgment was eventually reversed on appeal.

Shortly after, yet another judgment by a court in Jackson, Mississippi, was filed against the NAACP. Jackson businessmen had sued the organization after NAACP members boycotted their stores. The NAACP was forced to post a cash bond in excess of $1.5 million or have its assets seized.

The NAACP had used the courts to advance the issue of civil rights. But now, the courts were threatening the organization's financial stability. Pressure increased on Roy Wilkins, then in his seventies, to step down, and it was eventually agreed that he would resign effective in 1977.

A NEW LEADER

When Benjamin Hooks became NAACP Executive Director on August 1, 1977, he faced an organization that was dealing not merely with financial concerns but also dwindling support. There had been nearly half a million members of the NAACP in the 1950s and 1960s, but by 1977 membership had diminished to about 200,000.

Hooks was determined to turn things around. His plan was to reorganize the NAACP, while continuing to focus on effecting change through litigation, legislation, and negotiation. He determined to focus on building new alliances with businesses and corporations, labor organizations, Jewish groups, and liberal organizations. He felt that the NAACP should focus on issues of concern outside the United States—for example, pressuring American businesses to withdraw from South Africa and to pressure the U.S. government to play a more active role in encouraging self-determination in that country.

As part of the effort to reorganize the NAACP, Hooks felt that two new departments should be created—one to, as promised, focus on the media; the other to liaise with churches to improve NAACP efforts at the local level. Just before assuming office, at the 68th NAACP Convention held in June 1977, Hooks delivered this fiery promise:

> The train is running toward freedom. We invite you to get on or off at your pleasure, but for God's sake don't stand on the track unless you want to be run down.

Hooks believed that one of the NAACP's priorities should be focusing on the problems African Americans were facing in cities. "When the rate of unemployment among black teenagers runs as high as 40 percent, there can be no salving of the wounds. There can be no move-ment forward," he said in an interview in *Newsweek*, noting that urban areas also presented the issues of quality education, busing, and so-called "white flight" (in which white residents were moving out of urban areas and into suburbs), all of which he wanted the NAACP to address.

Hooks viewed many of these crises in a global, not merely national, context. "If we don't solve this race prob-lem," he said, "this country isn't going to ever rest in peace. Particularly when we have ferment in Africa, in India, in all of Asia, where colored people outnumber white people in this world. America ought to be the pre-eminent moral leader of this world. And the major reason we don't occu-py that [position] is because of the way we've handled the race question."

Under Hooks's leadership, the NAACP raised the necessary funds to pay off the debts incurred by the court cases in Mississippi, in large part thanks to contri-butions from the Rockefeller Foundation. But in January 1978, at almost the same time as it was announced that the NAACP was financially solvent, Hooks considered resigning. He had already run into conflict with members of the NAACP Board of Directors over several policy decisions. Hooks had requested additional money to hire a chief aide and to increase the salaries of certain key staff members. The board refused. Hooks also disagreed with an NAACP policy paper that criticized President Jimmy Carter's administration for the strict standards of its energy pro-gram which, the report claimed, would lead to layoffs in industry and lead to inflation that would more severely affect minorities.

In fact, conflicts with the board of directors marked Hooks's early years with the NAACP. In 1983, chair of the NAACP's board of directors, Margaret Bush Wilson, suddenly suspended Hooks following a quarrel over organizational policy. Wilson also charged Hooks with mismanagement, but the charge could not be proven. In fact, the 64-member board was outraged that Wilson had suspended Hooks without seeking the board's approval, and in turn fired her and reinstated Hooks.

For three more years, conflict rocked the NAACP. Three different people served as the chair of the board of directors. During this period, Hooks focused on liaising with major corporations and was able to obtain such large sums as a grant of one billion dollars from the American Gas Association to create economic opportunities, including jobs, for African Americans.

As the board of directors became more stable, Hooks was able to press ahead with his plans to revitalize the NAACP. Working from the NAACP's office in Baltimore, Maryland, he focused beyond simply the present to the organization's future. One of his goals was to ensure that the NAACP was reaching out to African-American youth and professionals. During his tenure, he oversaw a doubling in the number of NAACP college chapters and an increase in overall membership to more than half a million people.

A LEADER'S LEGACY

With Benjamin Hooks as its executive director, the NAACP was active on many fronts—at the local, national, and international level. The organization focused with increased vigor on voting rights and on judicial policy, while remaining vigilant about issues involving equal opportunity. In 1981, the NAACP was at the forefront of political lobbying to extend the Voting Rights Act for another 25 years. Hooks's efforts to build links with corporations helped lead to the establishment of the Fair Share Program, which provided increased opportunities for African Americans.

In 1982, the NAACP's campaign to encourage African Americans to vote led to the registration of more than 850,000 voters. The organization also lobbied President Ronald Reagan to prevent racially segregated Bob Jones University from receiving tax breaks from the U.S. government. In fact, many of President Reagan's conservative policies placed new roadblocks in NAACP efforts to further the evolution of the civil rights movement. The Reagan administration rejected many of the concepts of affirmative action, redress of discriminatory practices unless intent could be proved, and compensation for the effects of discrimination unless victims could be identified. This shift in policy affected educational opportunities, programs receiving federal funds, housing, employment, and even voting.

In 1984, Executive Director Hooks led a march on Washington to protest the Reagan administration's policies that Hooks believed threatened civil rights. Approximately 125,000 people participated in the march.

Reagan's nomination of Judge Robert Bork to the Supreme Court sparked another NAACP lobbying campaign. Finding fault with Bork's judicial record and fearing that his presence on the Supreme Court could pose a threat to much that had been achieved by civil rights activists, the NAACP launched a campaign to defeat Bork's nomination. More than 100,000 people participated in a 1989 Silent March to protest Bork's nomination. Bork ultimately received the highest negative vote ever recorded for a U.S. Supreme Court nominee.

In 1986, Benjamin Hooks received the Spingarn Medal—an award presented by the NAACP to honor African Americans who have achieved a high level of excellence in their chosen fields. Hooks ensured that the NAACP was active in providing equal opportunities for African Americans through programs like affirmative action, lobbying for increased federal aid to cities, and better educational facilities. But he was quick to note that African Americans must be willing to help themselves. At a 1990 gathering of NAACP convention delegates, Hooks noted that middle-class and wealthy African Americans had a responsibility to help those less fortunate: "It's time today ... to bring it out of the closet: no longer can we proffer polite, explicable reasons why Black America cannot do more for itself. I'm calling for a moratorium on excuses. I challenge Black America today—all of us—to set aside our alibis."

THE 1990s

After more than a decade at the head of the NAACP, Hooks still saw many challenges and opportunities facing the NAACP. While speaking at the Massachusetts Institute of Technology (MIT) in January 1991 for a ceremony honoring Dr. Martin Luther King Jr., Hooks noted that racism was still a factor in universities, in political campaigns, and in the military. He underscored the need for affirmative action to increase both the numbers of African Americans, Latinos, Native Americans, and women in colleges and graduate schools.

He saw the NAACP's challenge in the 1990s as fourfold: to build coalitions, to eliminate envy and jealousy, to exhibit a sense of pride, and to remember God.

> "I make no excuses whatsover," he said, "... for the fact that this nation needs affirmative action. If it spent all of these years keeping black and women out, it's high time that [it] spent some time bringing them in... In spite of the heartaches and disappointments, there is still hope. In spite of all we've gone through, I rejoice that when I go to Los Angeles, California to see the mayor, I walk into the office of a black man.... We've come a long way—seven thousand elected black officials, a million black young people in post-secondary education—these are the bright spots, things that make me happy."

Hooks saw opportunity in the political accomplishments he cited, but he knew first-hand that racism was still at work. Early in 1990, the country had been rocked by a series of bombings targeting civil rights leaders. Hooks and his family had been targeted. President George H.W. Bush wrote to Hooks on January 2, 1990, noting his outrage and determination to bring a halt to the violence:

> The recent bombings make it clear we have not totally beaten back the evils of bigotry and racial prejudice. We cannot let up in the fight against racism. Please assure your members I will see that the Federal Government does not let up as it works to bring the perpetrators of these hideous crimes to justice.

Hooks later met with President Bush to discuss the increased racial tension. While he was assured of the president's support for action against the racially motivated bombing, Hooks pressed further, urging the president to take greater action to combat inner-city poverty and increase funds available for public education. He was disappointed that the administration did not take the kind of sweeping action he had proposed in these areas.

Hooks was also alarmed by the increasingly open face of racism. In 1991, David Duke—an admitted racist and former leader of the KKK—began a campaign for the U.S. Senate seat in Louisiana. The NAACP was quick to respond, launching a voter registration campaign that resulted in a 76 percent turnout of African-American voters. Duke was defeated.

In 1991, the NAACP was drawn into another political controversy, this one involving the confirmation hearings for Clarence Thomas, an African American who had been nominated by President Bush to serve on the Supreme Court. Thomas had previously served as head of the Equal Employment Opportunity Commission (EEOC), and one of his employees there, Anita Hill, gave testimony during Thomas's confirmation hearings that he had sexually harassed her. At the time of the hearings, Hill had left the EEOC and was serving as a professor of law, and her testimony was considered very credible.

The NAACP also felt that Thomas should not be appointed, and on September 20, 1991, Benjamin Hooks appeared before the congressional committee overseeing the hearings to give his own testimony. Hooks noted that the NAACP had previously opposed Thomas's nomination to the EEOC and opposed him as a Supreme Court justice because of his record of opposition to affirmative action:

> We all know affirmative action is a strong, unwavering national policy of inclusion in the vital pursuit of

everyday necessities—a home, an education, a job, a promotion. In other words, all that affirmative action requires is a fair break. It is not a quota system nor, in its highest application, a preference system. It guards sharply against a quota system, and we believe that these are the fundamental guarantees of the American Constitution. And yet Judge Thomas has consistently expressed his steadfast opposition.

Hooks noted that the NAACP opposed Thomas for his opposition to "class-based relief," for his speeches against the Voting Rights Act, and for his opposition to several court cases designed to desegregate schools. Despite the testimony of Hooks, of Hill, and others, Judge Thomas was ultimately appointed to the Supreme Court.

CALL FOR CHANGE

In 1991, some younger members of the NAACP began to call for Hooks to step down. They felt that, after nearly 14 years at the head of the NAACP, the 66-year-old Hooks was losing touch with the needs of contemporary African Americans.

An article in the *Akron Beacon Journal* described the NAACP as a "dinosaur whose national leadership is still living in the glory days of the civil rights movement." The article even quoted the young head of an Ohio chapter of the NAACP, Dr. Frederick Zak, who said, "There is a tendency by some of the older people to romanticize the struggle—especially the marching and the picketing and the boycotting and the going to jail."

The criticism weighed heavily on Hooks. By now a great-grandfather, Hooks was feeling a renewed sense of spirituality, and he hoped to lead the NAACP in that direction. He believed that violence in the African-American community could be addressed by a new focus on building stable, nuclear families. He felt a responsibility to the NAACP and promised to stay on to lead it into the 21st century. But only a few months later, Benjamin Hooks decided to resign.

6

Reaching for New Promises

"Martin Luther King, Jr. and Nelson Mandela are genuine heroes of the long, long struggle for freedom. In the particular circumstances of their lives and times they fought to bring new freedom to black men and women. Truly, though, their cause was the cause of all humanity.

Why do we say that King and Mandela are heroes? High among our reasons, we place their sheer physical courage. That courage led King to embrace the nonviolent struggle, to endure the dogs and hoses, the many jailings, the physical assaults. It led him to live the maxim, 'Danger is the inseparable companion of honor.'

Mandela's courage involved armed resistance. He knew in undertaking his course what might be required of him, but he did not flinch or falter. He never surrendered his dignity.

We also find the intellectual capabilities of these
two men to be of heroic proportions. Learned men,
they did not use intellect as a trophy, but as a weapon.
Finally, we find them heroic because one was and the
other is a man at ease with his own humanity."
—Benjamin Hooks,
A compendium of thoughts and excerpts
from the Executive Director of the NAACP
on the significant issues of our time

Benjamin Hooks announced his decision to retire as
executive director of the NAACP in February 1992. He
was sixty-seven years old, and the demands and pressure
weighed too heavily on him. He was discouraged by the
claims that he and other more senior leaders of the organization were out of step with the times, but he knew that
new challenges faced the NAACP and believed that the
organization was now stable enough to survive a change in
leadership.

Several candidates were considered to replace Hooks in
the executive director role. In the end, the board of directors selected someone quite different from Benjamin
Hooks—Benjamin F. Chavis, Jr. Chavis was chosen in part
because of his youth—the board hoped to attract young
members by appointing a young activist to head the organization. Chavis was a controversial choice—he had been
imprisoned for four years as a result of what ultimately
proved to be a false conviction in 1972 on charges of con-
spiring to commit arson in Wilmington, North Carolina.

Chavis proved a much more militant leader than
Hooks. He aligned himself more closely with separatist
groups like the Nation of Islam, whose actions and philos-

Benjamin Hooks retired from his position as executive director of the National Association for the Advancement of Colored People (NAACP) in February 1992, amidst calls for new and younger leadership. Hooks's leadership position was filled, briefly, by scandal-plagued Benjamin Chavis, Jr., who has since been replaced by a new president and CEO, Kweisi Mfume.

ophy had previously been the subject of criticism from the NAACP, in part for its anti-semitic policies. Chavis also invited the controversial head of the Nation of Islam, Louis Farrakhan, to a leadership conference, prompting many NAACP members to withdraw their support for the organization.

Chavis's background had made it clear that his leadership of the NAACP would be more confrontational and more militant than that of Hooks. A conflict quickly arose between those who felt that Chavis had veered away from the historic mission of the NAACP to those who supported his ideas and policies, believing that they would invigorate the NAACP and encourage young African Americans to become members.

Chavis was able to increase the number of young people joining the NAACP, and his policy of meeting with gang leaders to discuss ways to curtail urban violence drew praise. Chavis also expanded the focus of the NAACP, coining terms like "environmental racism" to point out how environmental protection was less strictly enforced in minority communities and protesting government policies that protected producers of commercial hazardous waste facilities whose actions impacted minority communities.

Chavis also spoke out on the North American Free Trade Agreement (NAFTA), supporting the 1992 treaty designed to gradually phase out the majority of trade barriers and tariffs on products and services passing from one North American country to another. In fact, his unauthorized statements supporting NAFTA's policies in the United States, Canada, and Mexico, made without first consulting the NAACP Board, drew criticism from many members of the NAACP.

While many disagreed with the NAACP's shift away from the more traditional mandates carried out under Hooks to the more militant stance under Chavis, it was not politics but finances that would ultimately bring an end to Chavis's leadership of the NAACP. The first signs of trouble came with increasing expenses. Because of dwindling membership numbers and increases in staff salaries, the NAACP's budget deficit increased steadily, soon rising to more than a million dollars.

Then, in 1994, it was learned that Chavis had used NAACP funds to pay for an out-of court settlement of a sexual harassment suit. The suit had been filed against Chavis by a female member of his NAACP staff. Chavis was quickly forced to resign as executive director. In 1996, Kweisi Mfume was named the president and CEO of the NAACP, serving as the organization's official spokesperson while simultaneously being responsible for all daily operations.

THE NAACP'S NEW DIRECTION

Kweisi Mfume represented a shift away from the more militant stance of Chavis and a return to the type of more traditional leadership that Benjamin Hooks exemplified. Mfume's West African name translates to "conquering son of kings," and his lifelong focus has been to shape public policy and impact society through public service. Prior to becoming leader of the NAACP, Mfume was elected to a seat on Baltimore's City Council, where he focused on diversifying Baltimore's municipal government and enhancing the development of minority-owned businesses. He also worked to divest municipal funds from any involvement in the apartheid government of South Africa.

In 1986, Mfume was elected to U.S. Congress. For ten years, he served on a wide range of committees, including the Banking and Financial Services Committee, the General Oversight and Investigations Subcommittee, the Committee on Education, and the Small Business Committee. He also served on the Ethics Committee and the Joint Economic Committee of the House and Senate, later becoming its chair. Mfume's congressional record reflected his commitment to advancing minority business ownership and civil rights legislation. He was a co-sponsor of the Americans with Disabilities Act and a co-sponsor of an amendment to the Civil Rights Bill of 1991 that helped expand the coverage of the act to include application to

U.S. citizens working for American companies overseas. He also helped to strengthen the Equal Credit Opportunity Law and amended the Community Reinvestment Act in the interest of minority financial institutions. While in Congress, he served as chairman of the Congressional Black Caucus and as the Caucus's Chair of the Task Force on Affirmative Action.

Mfume gave up his congressional seat after being unanimously elected to the position of President and CEO of the NAACP on February 20, 1996. He quickly set to work to shape a new agenda for the NAACP, summing up the plan in six points: civil rights; political empowerment; educational excellence; economic development; health; and youth outreach.

Like Hooks, Mfume also had a background in broadcasting, having spent 13 years in radio and nine years hosting the television program *The Bottom Line*. He continued Hooks's emphasis of ensuring greater opportunities for minorities in broadcasting.

By 2000, Mfume had overseen a turnaround in NAACP finances. The organization's debt had been retired, and it was enjoying a budget surplus. Voter awareness efforts had resulted in the largest African-American voter turnout in 20 years.

CIVIL RIGHTS SPEAKER

With the end of Hooks's leadership, the NAACP had temporarily faltered before finding a clear sense of leadership and direction. But while the organization he had led shifted focus, Hooks had remained true to his own personal mandate to speak out on issues affecting civil rights. His compelling speaking style and historical connection to the civil rights movement made him a popular speaker on civil rights issues. He also joined the faculty of the University of

Memphis as a professor of political science.

As national issues affecting civil rights policies arose, Hooks continued to speak out. He was frequently invited to address groups for their Martin Luther King, Jr. Day celebrations. At one such ceremony at the University of Michigan in January 1995, Hooks was invited to give the keynote address at the university's Martin Luther King Jr. Day Symposium.

The speech he gave was typical of Hooks's view that the struggle for equality and racial justice was far from over. Hooks believed that danger lay in the complacency that had become typical in certain communities. There was a sense that the civil rights movement had ended, its goals achieved.

Hooks noted that Americans must not become complacent in their struggle for racial justice. Progress had been made, but there was more work to be accomplished—work that required the effort and "the kind of faith that Martin Luther King had." Hooks reflected on King's dream of a unified America, saying, "I am convinced that you may kill the dreamer but you cannot kill the dream."

STANDING UP TO THE KLAN

In 1998, Hooks's effort to support the vision of Martin Luther King, Jr. and his ongoing campaign to stand up against the forces of oppression came together in his hometown of Memphis. In January 1998, as Memphis prepared to begin a three-month celebration of King's legacy on the thirtieth anniversary of his death, the Ku Klux Klan chose to stage an appearance in Memphis to demonstrate its challenge to the Federal holiday honoring King.

Approximately 50 members of an Indiana branch of the Ku Klux Klan staged a rally on the steps of the county courthouse in Memphis. Memphis's mayor, Willie

Herenton—the city's first African-American mayor—urged residents to stay away from the Klan protest. Nonetheless, a crowd of about 1,500 protestors—both white and African American—staged a counterprotest next to the Klan rally.

Klan speakers mocked Dr. King's famous "I Have a Dream" speech and called for a return to racial segregation. When crowd members from both sides began to taunt the 200 policemen gathered to prevent violence, the policemen responded with pepper spray and tear gas, attempting to break up the anti-Klan protest. The police officers stated that they had spotted gang members in the anti-Klan crowd, and that they had tried to break down a police barrier that had been erected to separate the Klan and anti-Klan rallies. Several storefront windows in the vicinity were broken, and more than two dozen people were arrested.

According to a *New York Times* report of the events, many of the businesses whose windows had been broken were African American-owned businesses. And those responsible were young African Americans carrying sticks.

Benjamin Hooks spoke out against the violence on both sides: "In my more than 40 years at the NAACP, it was a rule of thumb that when the Klan rallies, you don't attempt a counterrally. Well-meaning people, who naively believe they can prove something, give others a mask to hide behind and trouble is inevitable."

SHOES OF IRON

In 2002, the seventy-six-year-old Hooks joined the law firm of Wyatt, Tarrant & Combs LLP. In addition to his duties as civil rights spokesperson and professor of political science, Hooks became "of counsel" to the prestigious Louisville, Kentucky-based firm, whose Memphis branch was one of the oldest and largest law firms in the city. Hooks's full-time position involved advising the firm's corporate clients on ways to ensure that they are not in violation of discrimination laws.

Hooks's background as author of many of the NAACP's studies on hiring diversity among legal firms and Wall Street firms, as well as his prominence as a civil rights spokesperson, made him an obvious choice for the position. The move had, in part, been initiated by Hooks. He was interested in once more becoming involved in the practice of law, but did not want to join a firm that would require a routine, daily involvement in legal business. He mentioned his interest to a friend, who happened to be an attorney with Wyatt, Tarrant & Combs.

Hooks learned that the firm included among its clients Berea College, the college that his grandmother had attended. And he did like the fact that the firm contained African-American partners.

"I've been a token and a first man long enough," Hooks noted. "Here they've already made a commitment."

Hooks's retirement from the NAACP was clearly not a slowing down, but merely a change to new opportunities and new challenges. His work as a professor and an attorney and as a spokesperson for civil rights issues, was demanding, but Hooks also continued to serve as pastor of the Greater Middle Baptist Church, and as vice president of Chapman Co., a minority-controlled investment banking firm. He also served as the president of the board of directors of the National Civil Rights Museum.

Benjamin Hooks's legacy is still being shaped. At the University of Memphis, the Benjamin L. Hooks Institute for Social Change was founded in 1996. The Hooks Institute is a research center designed to support urban research and to honor Benjamin Hooks's leadership role in the civil rights movement. The Institute has initiated research, teaching, and outreach programs designed to create a greater understanding of the civil rights movement, race relations, public education, and economic development. The Institute sponsors education initiatives on civil rights and civic responsibilities for public schools; sponsors the Hooks Lectures, a series of talks by prominent scholars, policy makers and community leaders designed to build stronger communities and promote racial justice; and sponsors the Hooks Symposia on Social Change, in which government officials, scholars, and community leaders meet with students and faculty at the University of Memphis to discuss the civil rights movement and its legacy. The Hooks Institute is also engaged in archiving Benjamin Hooks's personal and professional papers, and developing a series of research and public events designed to offer a major appraisal of the significance of *Brown* v. *Board of Education.*

Benjamin Hooks's legacy stretches across many facets of American life. Throughout the many phases of his professional career, he remained focused on the basic principle that equal opportunity and justice should be available to all Americans, regardless of the color of their skin.

In 2000, speaking in Greensboro, North Carolina, to an audience of more than 1,500 delegates from southeastern branches of the NAACP at their 48th annual regional conference, Hooks noted that they could look back with pride, but they should continue to press ahead, as well.

"I don't think any other race could have gone through what we've been through and walked through it with heads still held high," he said. "...When you think about it, we've come a long way because we've had shoes of iron. [But] the fight ain't over yet."

Chronology

1925 Benjamin Lawson Hooks is born in Memphis.

1941 Hooks graduates from Booker T. Washington High School in Memphis; enrolls at LeMoyne College.

1943 Hooks is drafted into the United States Army.

1946 Hooks enrolls at DePaul University Law School in Chicago.

1948 Hooks receives his J.D. from DePaul and returns to Memphis to practice law.

1949 Hooks establishes a law practice; meets Frances Dancy.

1951 Hooks and Dancy are married.

1954 Hooks runs an unsuccessful campaign to become State Legislator.

1956 Hooks becomes pastor of Middle Baptist Church in Memphis.

1959 Hooks runs an unsuccessful campaign to become Juvenile Court Judge.

1961 Hooks is appointed Assistant Public Defender of Shelby County.

1963 Hooks makes second attempt to become Juvenile Court Judge; fails to win election.

1964 Hooks becomes pastor of Greater New Mount Moriah Baptist Church in Detroit.

1965 Hooks becomes first African-American criminal court judge in Tennessee history.

1968 Hooks resigns his seat on criminal court bench.

1972 Hooks becomes the first African-American appointee to the Federal Communications Commission.

1977 Hooks becomes Executive Director of the NAACP.

1983 Hooks is suspended following a policy argument with the chair of the NAACP board of directors. He is quickly reinstated by other members of the board.

1986 Hooks is awarded the Spingairn Medal.

1990 Hooks is a target of a racially motivated bombing attempt.

1992 Hooks announces his retirement as Executive Director of the NAACP.

1993 Hooks becomes President of Board of Directors of National Civil Rights Museum.

1996 Benjamin L. Hooks Institute for Social Change is founded at the University of Memphis.

2002 Hooks joins Wyatt, Terrant & Combs, L.L.P.

Bibliography

Amaker, Norman C. *Civil Rights and the Reagan Administration.* Washington, D.C.: The Urban Institute Press, 1988.

Buckley, Gail. *American Patriots: The Story of Blacks in the Military from the Revolution to Desert Storm.* New York: Random House, 2001.

Cartwright, Joseph H. *The Triumph of Jim Crow: Tennessee Race Relations in the 1880s.* Knoxville, Tenn.: The University of Tennessee Press, 1976.

Covington, Owen. "Challenges Great, But God Provides," *High Point Enterprise,* March 17, 2000.

Fairclough, Adam. *To Redeem the Soul of America: The Southern Christian Leadership Conference and Martin Luther King, Jr.* Atlanta: The University of Georgia Press, 1987.

Hutchins, Francis S. *Berea College: The Telescope and the Spade.* New York: The Newcomen Society, 1963.

Kasher, Steven. *The Civil Rights Movement: A Photographic History, 1954–68.* New York: Abbeville Press, 1996.

Lamon, Lester C. *Black Tennesseans: 1900–1930.* Knoxville, Tenn.: The University of Tennessee Press, 1977.

Levy, Peter B., ed. *Let Freedom Ring: A Documentary History of the Modern Civil Rights Movement.* New York: Praeger, 1992.

Litwack, Leon F. *Trouble in Mind: Black Southerners in the Age of Jim Crow.* New York: Alfred A. Knopf, 1998.

Margo, Robert A. *Race and Schooling in the South, 1880–1950.* Chicago: The University of Chicago Press, 1990.

Miller, William D. *Memphis During the Progressive Era.* Memphis, Tenn.: The Memphis State University Press, 1957.

Moritz, Charles, ed. *Current Biography Yearbook 1978.* New York: H.W. Wilson, Co., 1978, pp. 198–202.

Mullen, Robert W. *Blacks in America's Wars: The Shift in Attitudes from the Revolutionary War to Vietnam.* New York: Pathfinder, 1973.

Peake, Thomas R. *Keeping the Dream Alive: A History of the Southern Christian Leadership Conferences from King to the 1980s.* New York: Peter Lang, 1987.

Perkins, Tommy. "Ex-NAACP Exec Joins Firm." *Memphis Business Journal.* February 15, 2002.

Rhym, Darren. *The NAACP.* Philadelphia. Chelsea House Publishers, 2003.

Rowan, Carl T. *Dream Makers, Dream Breakers.* Boston: Little, Brown & Co., 1993.

Segal, Geraldine R. *Blacks in the Law.* Philadelphia: University of Pennsylvania Press, 1983.

Shannon, Elaine. "The New Voice of the NAACP." *Newsweek,* November 22, 1976, p. 46.

Smith, Michael David. *Race versus Robe: The Dilemma of Black Judges.* Port Washington, N.Y.: Associated Faculty Press, 1983.

Thernstrom, Abigail M. *Whose Votes Count? Affirmative Action and Minority Voting Rights.* Cambridge, Mass.: Harvard University Press, 1987.

Thomson, Elizabeth A. "Echoing King, Hooks Also Sees Hope." *Tech Talk,* January 30, 1991.

Weatherford, Carole Boston. *Great African-American Lawyers.* Berkeley Heights, N.J.: Enslow Publishers, 2003.

Wilkins, Roy and Tom Mathews. *Standing Fast: The Autobiography of Roy Wilkins.* New York: The Viking Press, 1982.

Wynn, Neil A. *The Afro-American and the Second World War.* New York: Homes & Meir, 1975.

Yellin, Emily. "A City Strives to Balance its Role in King Legacy." *New York Times,* January 9, 1998.

Bibliography

www.benhooks.memphis.edu

www.berea.edu

www.bushlibrary.tamu.edu/papers/1990/90010202.html

www.campnelson.org

www.ket.org/underground/history/

www.kytales.com/kyana/britt.html

www.law.cornell.edu/constitution/

www.lexisnexis.com/academic/guides/african_american/sclc/sclc1.asp

www.memory.loc.gov/ammem/aap/aaphome.html

www.multied.com/bio/people/wilkins.html

www.museum.tv/archives/

www.naacp.org

www.nps.gov.ncro/anti/emancipation.html

www.nyking.org/celebration/keynote_hooks.html

www.pbs.org/weta/apr/

www.people.memphis.edu/~polisci/hookbio.htm

www.people.virginia.edu/~govdoc/thomas/0920a03.html

www.pub.umich.edu/daily/1997/jan/01-27-97/edit.edit3.html

www.templeton-interactive.com/lest8a.htm

www.tnstate.edu/library/digital/hooks.htm

Further Reading

Buckley, Gail. *American Patriots: The Story of Blacks in the Military from the Revolution to Desert Storm.* New York: Random House, 2001.

Dudley, William, ed. *The 1960s.* San Diego: Greenhaven Press, 2000.

Kasher, Steven. *The Civil Rights Movement: A Photographic History, 1954-68.* New York: Abbeville Press, 1996.

Levine, Ellen. *Freedom's Children: Young Civil Rights Activists Tell Their Own Stories.* New York: G.P. Putnam's Sons, 1993.

Rhym, Darren. *The NAACP.* Philadelphia: Chelsea House Publishers, 2003.

Time-Life Books. *African Americans Voices of Triumph: Leadership.* New York: Time Life Inc., 1993.

Weatherford, Carole Boston. *Great African-American Lawyers.* Berkeley Heights, N.J.: Enslow Publishers, 2003.

Wilkins, Roy and Mathews, Tom. *Standing Fast: The Autobiography of Roy Wilkins.* New York: The Viking Press, 1982.

Related Web Sites

www.benhooks.memphis.edu

www.civilrights.org

www.memory.loc.gov/ammem/aap/aaphome.html

www.naacp.org

www.pbs.org/weta/apr/

www.thecrisismagazine.com

www2.una.edu/mjohnson/afam.htm

Index

Index

Index

Index

Index

Picture Credits

About the Author

Heather Lehr Wagner is a writer and editor. She earned an M.A. in government from the College of William and Mary and a B.A. in political science from Duke University. She is the author of more than twenty books, including biographies of *George Washington, Thomas Jefferson,* and *John Adams* in Chelsea House's *Great American Presidents* series.